olive
magazine

101 SMART SUPPERS

D0808481

1 3 5 7 9 10 8 6 4 2

Published in 2007 by BBC Books, an imprint of Ebury Publishing

Ebury Publishing is a division of the Random House Group

First published 2007
Copyright © 2007
All photographs © *olive* magazine 2007

The Random House Group Limited Reg. No. 954009

Addresses for companies within the Random House Group can be found at
www.randomhouse.co.uk

A CIP catalogue record for this book is available from the British Library

The Random House Group Limited makes every effort to ensure that the
papers used in our books are made from trees that have been legally
sourced from well-managed and credibly certified forests. Our paper
procurement policy can be found at www.randomhouse.co.uk

Commissioning Editor: Vivien Bowler   Project Editor: Deirdre O'Reilly
Designer: Kathryn Gammon   Production Controller: Peter Hunt

Printed and bound in Italy by LEGO SpA
Colour origination by Dot Gradations Ltd, UK

ISBN-13: 978 0 563 49397 6

101 SMART SUPPERS

slick ideas for weeknights

Editor
Lulu Grimes

BOOKS

Contents

Introduction 6

Introduction

There is no reason why after-work supper shouldn't be an exciting meal every day, achievable in 30 minutes or less and without the bother of chasing down hard-to-find ingredients. Weekends, on the other hand, are made for shopping and cooking, so we have included a handful of recipes to stretch the adventurous cook, though you'll still have them on the table in under an hour.

At *olive* we believe you deserve to eat well every day, so all of the 101 recipes chosen by the *olive* food team for this book are imaginative, satisfying and easy, such as *Chicken Caesar salad* pictured opposite (see page 52 for the recipe), as well as being smart enough to serve to your most discerning foodie friends.

There are recipes suited to each season and mood, whether you are after a light salad, warming soup, comforting stew or show-off steak. Every one of them is the kind of recipe that you will want to cook again and again.

As always, all the recipes have been thoroughly tested in the *olive* kitchen to make sure that they taste fabulous and work for you first time.

Lulu Grimes
olive magazine

Notes and Conversions

NOTES ON THE RECIPES

• Where possible, we use humanely reared meats, free-range chickens and eggs, and unrefined sugar.

• Eggs are large unless stated otherwise. Pregnant women, elderly people, babies and toddlers, and anyone who is unwell should avoid eating raw and partially cooked eggs.

APPROXIMATE WEIGHT CONVERSIONS

• All the recipes in this book are listed with metric measurements.

• Cup measurements, which are used by cooks in Australia and America, have not been listed here as they vary from ingredient to ingredient. Please use kitchen scales to measure dry/solid ingredients.

OVEN TEMPERATURES

gas	°C	fan °C	°F	description
¼	110	90	225	Very cool
½	120	100	250	Very cool
1	140	120	275	Cool or slow
2	150	130	300	Cool or slow
3	160	140	325	Warm
4	180	160	350	Moderate
5	190	170	375	Moderately hot
6	200	180	400	Fairly hot
7	220	200	425	Hot
8	230	210	450	Very hot
9	240	220	475	Very hot

SPOON MEASURES

• Spoon measurements are level unless otherwise specified.

• 1 teaspoon (tsp) = 5ml

• 1 tablespoon (tbsp) = 15ml

• 1 Australian tablespoon = 20ml (cooks in Australia should measure 3 teaspoons where 1 tablespoon is specified in a recipe)

APPROXIMATE LIQUID CONVERSIONS

metric	imperial	US
60ml	2fl oz	¼ cup
125ml	4fl oz	½ cup
175ml	6fl oz	¾ cup
225ml	8fl oz	1 cup
300ml	10fl oz/½ pint	1¼ cups
450ml	16fl oz	2 cups/1 pint
600ml	20fl oz/1 pint	2½ cups
1 litre	35fl oz/1¾ pints	1 quart

Please note that an Australian cup is 250ml, ¾ cup is 190ml, ½ cup is 125ml, ¼ cup is 60ml.

20-minute minestrone

20 minutes

onion 1, sliced

olive oil

chopped tomatoes 400g tin

mixed chopped vegetables 250g pack,
    fresh or frozen

courgette 1, sliced

vegetable stock cube, powder or fresh,
    made up to 1.5 litres

cannelini or flageolet beans 400g tin

pesto to serve

■ Fry the onion in a little oil for 2 minutes, add the tomatoes and cook for a minute and then add the veg and stock. Bring to a boil and simmer for 5 minutes, then add the beans and simmer for another 5 minutes. Season and serve with a tablespoon of pesto on top. **Serves 2**

One of those bags of ready-prepared veg makes this nice and speedy. Cut any larger chunks in half or quarters.

Griddled courgette salad with mozzarella and mint

20 minutes

courgettes 6 medium, thinly sliced lengthways

olive oil

mozzarella cheese 3 balls, torn into bite-size pieces

pine nuts 3 tbsp, toasted

preserved (or pickled) lemon 1, rind finely chopped (look for Belazu in supermarkets) or grated zest of 1 lemon

mint leaves a small bunch

DRESSING

extra-virgin olive oil 6 tbsp

lemons 2, juiced

clear honey 1 tsp

red chillies 1–2, deseeded and finely chopped or sliced

■ Brush the courgettes with olive oil and cook in batches on a heated griddle pan for about 2 minutes each side or until just tender. Transfer each batch to a warmed plate and cover while you cook the rest.

■ Combine all the dressing ingredients in a bowl and season with salt. Divide the courgette, mozzarella, pine nuts, preserved lemon and mint leaves among 6 serving plates. Spoon over the dressing.

Serves 6

Use a griddle pan if you have one, otherwise a frying pan will do just as well.

Bacon, bean and pasta soup

30 minutes

rindless streaky bacon 8 rashers, chopped
leeks 2, halved and sliced
carrots 4, halved lengthways and sliced
mixed beans 400g tin, drained and rinsed
chicken stock fresh, cube or concentrate,
    made up to 1 litre
tomato purée 2 tbsp
small pasta shapes 50g
flat-leaf parsley a handful, chopped
Parmesan cheese grated, to serve

■ Fry the bacon in a large non-stick pan (it will cook in its own fat) until golden, then add the leeks and carrots and cook for about 5 minutes until softened. Tip in the beans, chicken stock, tomato purée and pasta, and simmer until the pasta is cooked. Stir through the parsley and serve in bowls topped with grated Parmesan.
Serves 4

If you can't get small pasta shapes easily, snap a handful of spaghetti into short lengths.

Mackerel, beetroot and potato salad with horseradish dressing

20–25 minutes

new potatoes 10 small
smoked mackerel 2 fillets
cooked beetroot 4 small, look for
ones that are vacuum-packed
rather than in vinegar
baby spinach 2 handfuls

DRESSING
horseradish cream 2 tbsp
lemon 1, juiced
natural yoghurt 1 small carton

■ Boil the potatoes until tender. Flake the mackerel into large chunks. Whisk the horseradish, lemon and yoghurt together. Quarter the beets. Pile the spinach on to plates and divide the warm potatoes and beetroot among them. Scatter the mackerel over and drizzle with the dressing. **Serves 2**

Smoked mackerel is available plain or peppered; either will work well for this.

Grilled crottin with pear and walnut salad

10 minutes

goat's cheese crottin 1, halved
    horizontally
salad leaves 2 handfuls
ripe pear 1, peeled and halved or
    quartered
walnut halves 10, toasted

DRESSING
sherry vinegar 1 tbsp
walnut oil 4 tbsp

■ Heat the grill to high and grill the cheese, cut-side up, until browned. Whisk together the dressing ingredients. In a bowl, toss the salad leaves, pear, walnuts and dressing, then arrange on 2 plates. Top each salad with the grilled cheese and serve. **Serves 2**

Crottins are small, squat, barrel-shape cheeses with a whitish (bloomy) rind. You can also use slices off a log.

Chilled cucumber and mint soup

20 minutes

cucumbers 2 large, peeled
butter 25g
garlic 1 clove, crushed
dry white wine 1 glass, about 150ml
chicken stock fresh, powder or cube,
    made up to 500ml
mint 1 bunch, leaves only
crème fraîche to serve

If you feel like making this more special,
float an ice cube set with mint leaves in
each bowl of soup.

■ Cut the cucumbers in half lengthways
and scoop out the seeds with a teaspoon.
Chop the flesh. Heat the butter in a
saucepan over a medium heat and fry
the cucumber (save a couple of spoonfuls
to top the soup) until it starts to soften a
little. Add the garlic and stir. Put a lid on
the pan, reduce the heat and cook for 5
minutes until the cucumber is quite soft.
■ Increase the heat, add the white wine
and bubble for a minute. Add the stock
and bring to the boil. Throw in the mint
and take the soup off the heat. Cool, then
whiz in a blender and season to taste.
■ Chill the soup until completely cold.
Serve with a sprinkling of cucumber,
a dollop of crème fraîche and minty ice
cubes (see tip left), if you like. **Serves 6**

Halloumi with chilli oil

20 minutes

halloumi cheese 2 × 250g packs, sliced
mixed leaf salad 2 bags
chilli oil 6 tbsp
chilli flakes ½ tsp
lemon wedges to serve

■ Heat a non-stick pan on a medium heat and cook the halloumi in batches for 3 minutes on each side or until golden – you won't need any oil.
■ Arrange the salad leaves on 6 individual plates and top with a couple of halloumi slices. Drizzle over the chilli oil and lightly scatter with the flakes. Squeeze on some lemon juice, if you like.
Serves 6

Serve this chilli-speckled fried cheese with a flat bread such as Arabic-style pitta bread that has been brushed with olive oil and baked.

Mozzarella and prosciutto salad with red pepper salsa

20 minutes

crusty bread 2 slices

olive oil

salad leaves a couple of handfuls of mixed leaves

mozzarella cheese 125g, torn up into bite-sized pieces

prosciutto 4–6 slices

SALSA

roasted red peppers 2 (from the deli counter or a jar)

cherry tomatoes a handful

balsamic vinegar 1 tbsp

olive oil

■ Make the croûtons by tearing the bread into rough chunks, then toss in a little olive oil with salt and black pepper. Crisp up on a baking sheet in a 180°C/fan 160°C/gas 4 oven for about 10 minutes.

■ To make the salsa, chop the peppers and mix them with the cherry tomatoes, balsamic vinegar, 1 tbsp olive oil and some seasoning.

■ Divide the salad leaves between 2 plates. Add the croûtons, mozzarella, ham and salsa. Season with black pepper.

Serves 2 as a light lunch

Store mozzarella in its liquid in the fridge. It should be fine for up to 4 days. If you want to keep it longer, replace the liquid by mixing spring water with a pinch of sea salt.

Panzanella with avocado

30 minutes

cherry tomatoes 16
olive oil
cucumber 1, peeled, halved, seeds
scooped out and sliced
country-style bread 4 slices, cut into 3cm
cubes
red onion 1, sliced
curly parsley 1 bunch, chopped
capers 1 tbsp, rinsed and drained
wine vinegar 2 tbsp
avocados 2

■ Heat the oven to 200°C/fan 180°C/gas 6.
Put the tomatoes on a baking tray with
a little olive oil and roast for 10 minutes.
■ Put the cucumber in a bowl with the
roasted tomatoes and bread. Add the
onion and parsley, along with the capers,
4 tbsp olive oil, the vinegar and some
seasoning. Mix well, cover and leave to
stand. Just before serving peel, stone and
slice the avocados. Arrange them on a
plate and serve topped with the
panzanella. **Serves 4**

Let the salad ingredients sit while you set
the table, so that all the flavours mingle
and the bread soaks up the dressing.

Cream of watercress soup

10 minutes

watercress 2 × 85g bags
spring onions 3, roughly chopped,
    including some of the green part
beef consommé 400g tin
milk 300ml
double cream 142ml carton
chives a few snipped as a finishing touch

■ Chuck out any particularly coarse stems of watercress. Put the rest in a food processor or blender with the spring onion and whiz till decimated. Scrape down the sides of the processor with a spatula and process again until as smooth as possible.

■ Add all the liquid ingredients and some seasoning. Process, taste and season again as necessary. Chill and serve very cold. Snip over some chives, if you fancy. **Serves 4**

You can exchange the watercress for the same quantity of a rocket-spinach-watercress mix if you prefer.

Griddled, marinated aubergine with feta and herbs

20 minutes

aubergines 2 large, sliced lengthways into ½cm-thick slices

olive oil

lemon 1, juiced

garlic 1 clove, crushed

feta cheese 200g, crumbled

flat-leaf parsley a large handful, finely chopped

coriander leaves a large handful, finely chopped

■ Heat a griddle or frying pan until very hot. Brush the aubergine with a little olive oil and griddle or fry in batches until soft and cooked through. Arrange on a platter.

■ Mix together the lemon and garlic with 5 tbsp olive oil and some seasoning, and drizzle over the aubergine. Let the flavours meld together for 5 minutes, then scatter over the feta and herbs and serve. **Serves 4**

Choose young, firm, shiny aubergines for this; older ones tend to be bitter.

Pink grapefruit and prawn salad with Thai dressing

20 minutes

pink grapefruits 2
prawns 250g, cooked and peeled
shallots 3, sliced
coriander leaves a small handful
mint leaves a small handful
peanuts 1 tbsp, toasted and
    roughly crushed

DRESSING
garlic 1 clove, crushed
red chilli 1, seeded and chopped
ginger 1cm piece, grated
fish sauce 4 tbsp (available in
    most supermarkets)
lime 1, juiced
light muscovado sugar 2 tbsp

■ Cut the grapefruits into segments over a bowl to catch any juice. Whisk all the dressing ingredients into the grapefruit juice and leave until the sugar has dissolved.

■ Mix the grapefruit segments with the prawns and shallots. Pour over the dressing and stir through the coriander and mint leaves. Serve scattered with the nuts. **Serves 6**

White grapefruit or pomelo (a large citrus fruit that is sweeter than a grapefruit) can also be used for this salad.

Roast beef platter with rocket and olives

10 minutes

---

cooked potatoes 200g, cubed
olive oil
watercress 1 handful
rocket 1 handful
mixed olives 2 tbsp
capers 1 tbsp, rinsed and drained
cold roast beef 200g, sliced
mozzarella cheese 300g, sliced

■ Fry the potato cubes in a little olive oil until crisp. Mix the salad leaves with the olives and capers. Dress with olive oil and season.

■ Arrange alternate slices of beef and mozzarella in 2 rows down the length of a platter. Mix the warm potatoes and salad and pile down the centre. **Serves 4**

Use a ball of fresh buffalo mozzarella or try bocconcini (mini mozzarella balls), which you can find in pouches or tubs in larger supermarkets.

Smoked salmon, chicory and walnut salad

7 minutes

smoked salmon about 150g, sliced

chicory use white or red varieties,
    finely sliced

mixed salad leaves a good handful
    per person, choose an interesting
    mix – watercress and rocket add
    pepperiness

walnut halves a handful, toasted in a
    dry frying pan

DRESSING

walnut oil 6 tbsp

sherry or red wine vinegar 2 tbsp

■ Arrange the smoked salmon on
4 plates. Mix the dressing ingredients
and add a little seasoning.

■ Mix the chicory and salad leaves
together, drizzle with the walnut-oil
dressing and toss. Pile the salad on top
of the salmon. Scatter with the toasted
walnut halves. Serves 4

The smokiness, texture and colour
of smoked salmon varies: oak- or
peat-smoked salmon can be quite dark
and strong tasting. Farmed salmon
has a high colour, and organic tends
to be paler.

Curly kale and meatball soup

40 minutes

olive oil

onions 2, finely sliced

curly kale 200g, roughly chopped

chicken stock cube, powder or fresh, made up to 1 litre

Pecorino or Parmesan cheese grated to make 4 tbsp

MEATBALLS

white bread 1 slice

milk 2 tbsp

minced pork 250g

egg yolk 1

flat-leaf parsley 2 tbsp, finely chopped

garlic ½ clove, crushed

Pecorino or Parmesan cheese grated to make 2 tbsp

oil for frying

■ Heat 3 tbsp olive oil in a heavy pot. Add the onion, season well and cook until brown and caramelised. Meanwhile, bring a large pan of salted water to boil. Cook the kale for 4 minutes. Rinse well in cold water and drain.

■ For the meatballs, soak the bread in the milk. Then break up the soaked bread with your fingers. Add the remaining meatball ingredients plus 1 tsp salt and mix well. Roll the mixture into marble-size balls. Fry the meatballs in oil in a separate pan for a few minutes until browned and cooked through.

■ When the onions are ready, add the stock, kale and meatballs and heat through. Ladle into bowls and spoon the cheese over each before serving. **Serves 4**

Curly kale adds a robust texture to soups. Shred it finely if you prefer a less chunky finish.

The best salade Niçoise

30 minutes

runner beans 100g, sliced

eggs 4

new potatoes 4 medium, cooked
and sliced

cherry tomatoes 8, halved

lettuce a handful of leaves

tuna (in brine or spring water) 400g,
drained and kept in large chunks

anchovy fillets 4

olives 16

olive oil

white wine vinegar 2 tbsp

■ Bring a pan of water to the boil, cook
the beans for 1 minute in boiling water,
lift out and refresh under cold, running
water. Turn down the heat, add the eggs
to the pan and simmer for 5–6 minutes
(or 3–4 minutes if you like the yolks really
runny). Cool under cold, running water.
When they're cool enough to handle,
drain, shell and cut into quarters.

■ In a large bowl mix together the
potatoes, tomatoes, beans, lettuce, tuna,
anchovies, olives, 4 tbsp olive oil, vinegar
and some seasoning, and carefully toss.
Serve topped with the egg. **Serves 4**

Hand-filleted and packed tuna has
a firm texture that stays in good-sized
chunks. Most supermarkets stock a
speciality brand, either in tins or jars.

Tuscan bean soup

30 minutes

olive oil
shallots 4, chopped
garlic 2 cloves, crushed
pancetta 200g, chopped
celery 2 sticks, diced
potatoes 2, peeled and diced
borlotti or haricot beans 1 tin (about 425g), rinsed and drained
chicken stock fresh, cube or powder, made up to 1 litre
bay leaf 1
fresh oregano 1 tsp, chopped
flat-leaf parsley a handful, chopped
extra-virgin olive oil to serve

■ Heat 2 tbsp olive oil in a large saucepan, add the shallots, garlic, pancetta, celery and potatoes and fry for 5 minutes. Add the beans, stock, bay leaf and oregano, bring to the boil and simmer for 15 minutes.

■ Season and add the parsley and serve drizzled with a little extra-virgin olive oil and warm crusty bread. **Serves 4**

Tinned beans come in varying textures; the better the quality, the better they seem to stand up to cooking.

Seared beef with rocket and Parmesan

15 minutes

sirloin steaks 2, fat trimmed, brushed
    with a little oil and seasoned
rocket 50g
cherry tomatoes a handful, halved
Parmesan cheese a handful of shavings

DRESSING
olive oil
white wine vinegar 1 tbsp
Dijon mustard 1 tbsp

■ Heat a griddle or frying pan until smoking hot and cook the steaks – 2 minutes per side for rare, 3 for medium. Leave to rest for 5 minutes.

■ Meanwhile, make the dressing by whisking together 3 tbsp olive oil, vinegar and mustard with some seasoning. Slice the steak into strips and toss together with the rocket, tomatoes and dressing. Top with some Parmesan shavings. **Serves 2**

You can use any steaks for this – just make sure they are thick enough to give you decent slices.

Miso broth with rice noodles and shiitake mushrooms

15 minutes

instant miso soup 3 × 8g sachets (Sanchi brand is good)
beansprouts 50g
shiitake mushrooms 4–6, thinly sliced
spring onions 2, thinly sliced
fine stir-fry rice noodles 50g
tofu or peeled and cooked prawns 100g
soy sauce to season
sesame oil to sprinkle

■ Put the miso-soup mix in a saucepan and add the beansprouts, shiitake mushrooms, spring onions and rice noodles.

■ Pour in 600ml boiling water and bring to a simmer, turn off the heat and set aside for about 4 minutes until the noodles are soft.

■ Ladle into 2 bowls. Top with the tofu or prawns and a splash of soy sauce and sesame oil. **Serves 2**

If you have miso paste in your cupboard, it will work just as well as the instant miso soup. Both are readily available from supermarkets.

Chicken in a bag with sage and buttered potatoes

35 minutes

potatoes 4 large, thinly sliced
butter
chicken breasts 4 skinless
sage ½ bunch
lemon 1, halved

■ Heat the oven to 200°C/fan 180°C/gas 6. Divide the potatoes among 4 parchment bags (available from supermarkets or make your own with baking parchment) and add a good knob of butter and some seasoning to each. Lay a chicken breast on top of the potato slices, add a sprig of sage, a squeeze of lemon juice and another knob of butter and seal the bag.
■ Put the bags on a baking tray and bake for 25–30 minutes until the potato feels soft. Split open and serve. **Serves 4**

Cooking potatoes along with other ingredients, rather than on their own as a side dish, means they absorb lots of flavour.

Crunchy coated chicken with lemon mayo

20 minutes

fresh breadcrumbs 150g
Parmesan cheese 25g, grated
lemon 1, zested and juiced, plus extra
    wedges to serve
chicken breast fillets 4 skinless, flattened
flour for dusting
egg 1, beaten
olive oil
mayonnaise 4 tbsp
fennel 1 bulb, finely sliced
radishes 1 bunch, finely sliced

■ Mix the breadcrumbs, Parmesan and lemon zest. Season. Dust the chicken with flour. Dip into the egg then the breadcrumb mix. Fry the chicken in 4 tbsp olive oil in batches for 3–4 minutes each side or until cooked through. Drain on kitchen paper.

■ Mix the mayo with half the lemon juice. Toss the fennel and radish in the rest of the lemon juice. Serve the chicken with the salad and lemon mayo. **Serves 4**

If you prefer not to fry the chicken, you can bake it in a 200°C/fan 180°C/gas 6 oven for about 12–15 minutes.

Chicken Caesar salad

15 minutes

baby gem lettuces 2–3
cooked chicken fillets 2, sliced
croûtons 75g
anchovy fillets 4, drained and
     thinly sliced
Caesar dressing 4 tbsp (Cardini's
     is good)
Parmesan cheese a handful of shavings

■ Break up the lettuce leaves and divide between 2 bowls. Add the chicken, croûtons and sliced anchovies. Drizzle 2 tbsp dressing over each salad, season and finish with Parmesan shavings.
Serves 2

This is also a good recipe for using up leftover roast chicken. You'll need a couple of good handfuls.

Lemon and caper chicken

15 minutes

---

oil and butter for frying
mini chicken fillets 350g pack (or use
  2 chicken breasts)
capers 2 tbsp, rinsed and drained
lemon 1, juiced
salad leaves to serve

■ Heat 1 tbsp oil and a knob of butter in a frying pan until sizzling. Add the fillets and cook for 2–3 minutes on each side or until golden and cooked through. Throw in the capers and lemon juice, and stir until warmed through. Serve on salad leaves. **Serves 2**

This recipe uses false fillets from the chicken breast (sold as mini fillets in packs), but you can use regular chicken breasts butterflied, that is, slit horizontally and opened out like a book.

Chilli chicken fajitas

30 minutes

---

olive oil
chicken breasts 2 skinless, cut into strips
hot chilli powder 2 tsp
onion 1, halved and sliced
red pepper 1, sliced
green beans 100g
chopped tomatoes 400g tin
coriander leaves a handful, chopped
**flour tortillas, soured cream and green
    salad** to serve

■ Heat 2 tbsp olive oil in a large pan. Throw in the chicken and quickly brown all over, then add the chilli powder and cook for a minute. Scoop out the chicken, then add the onion and red pepper to the pan and cook until softened. Tip in the green beans, tomatoes and the chicken. Cover and simmer for 15 minutes.

■ Stir through the coriander and roll in warm tortillas with a dollop of soured cream. Serve with green salad. **Serves 2**

Warm the tortillas (before serving) by wrapping them in foil and putting them in a medium oven.

Spiced chicken with red onion and couscous salad

30 minutes

chicken breasts 4, skin on
harissa paste 2–3 tbsp
olive oil
couscous 300g
red onion 1, sliced thinly
chicken stock cube, powder or fresh,
    made up to 350ml, at boiling point
lemon 1, zested and juiced
tomatoes 2, chopped
feta cheese 200g, crumbled
mint a small bunch, roughly chopped

■ Heat the grill to medium. Slash the chicken and rub with the harissa. Put on a baking sheet skin-side down. Drizzle with olive oil and grill for 10 minutes, turning halfway through, until the chicken is cooked, and the skin is crisp.

■ Meanwhile, put the couscous in a large bowl with the red onion and pour over the stock. Cover and leave to stand until the stock has been absorbed (about 5 minutes). Fluff up with a fork, then stir in the lemon zest and juice, tomato, feta, mint and 2 tbsp olive oil. Serve with the chicken. **Serves 4**

Harissa can be bought in delis and most supermarkets – look out for Belazu rose harissa.

Parmesan and prosciutto chicken with saffron risotto

30 minutes

chicken breasts 2 skinless
Parmesan cheese 50g, shaved
prosciutto or Parma ham 2 slices
saffron risotto mix 1 packet (Gallo brand
   is good)
baby spinach leaves a large handful,
   washed

■ Heat the oven to 200°C/fan 180°C/gas 6. Use a sharp knife to cut lengthways through the fattest part of the chicken breast to make a pocket. Stuff the Parmesan in the pockets, then wrap a slice of prosciutto round each. Put the wrapped chicken breasts on a baking tray and bake for 12–14 minutes until cooked through.

■ Meanwhile, cook the risotto following packet instructions, using 50ml less water than suggested. When it's done, stir in the spinach: it will wilt and give up enough juice to make up the shortfall in water. Let the chicken breasts rest for 3 minutes, then slice crossways into 4 or 5 slices. Serve the risotto in deep dishes topped with the chicken. **Serves 2**

Saffron risotto mix can be substituted with 200g risotto rice, a pinch of saffron and 800–900ml stock or water.

Flattened chicken with courgettes

40 minutes

chicken breasts 6 skinless
extra-virgin olive oil
lemon 1, juice and zest
basil a small handful of leaves, torn
new potatoes 500g
butter
courgettes 12 baby or 6 small, cut
    into ribbons
green beans 300g, trimmed

■ Slice the breasts in half through the middle, leaving them joined along one side then lay out between 2 pieces of clingfilm. Bash flat with a rolling pin and put in a bowl with 5 tbsp olive oil, lemon juice, zest and most of the basil.

■ Boil the potatoes until cooked through then gently crush with a little butter and season. Steam the courgettes and beans for 2–3 minutes until tender. Griddle or fry the chicken for 4–6 minutes on each side until just cooked. Serve with the vegetables. Pour over any juices and sprinkle with the remaining basil. **Serves 6**

The easiest way to ribbon courgettes is by running a potato peeler down their length.

Chicken with olives and tomatoes

30 minutes

rosemary 1 sprig, chopped
onion 1 large, sliced
garlic 2 cloves, sliced
new potatoes 500g small, quartered
olive oil
chicken pieces 8–10 thighs and
    drumsticks, skin on
baby plum or cherry tomatoes 500g
dry white wine 300ml
chicken stock fresh, cube or concentrate
    made up to 300ml
olives 150g, drained
basil a small bunch, torn

■ Heat the oven to 220°C/fan 200°C/gas 7. Toss the first four ingredients in a roasting tray in 2 tbsp oil and cook for 25 minutes. Fry the chicken in 2 tbsp oil until browned and almost cooked through. Add to the tin for the last 10 minutes of cooking along with the tomatoes, wine, stock and olives. Scatter with basil and serve. **Serves 4**

You can cook the chicken in with the veg from the start, but you'll need to give the whole lot 45 minutes.

Lemon chicken with spaghetti

30 minutes

spaghetti or linguine 400g
lemons 2 unwaxed
chicken breasts 4, skin on
lemon thyme 1 bunch
olive oil
white wine 100ml

Spaghetti or linguine always look
elegant, but you can use penne
or another pasta shape for this.

■ Cook the spaghetti in a large pan of
boiling water, following packet
instructions. Drain and return to the pan.
Meanwhile, cut 1 lemon into 12 thin
slices; zest and juice the remaining
lemon. Carefully, lift one side of the skin
off the chicken breast and slide 3 lemon
slices and a few sprigs of the lemon
thyme underneath. Smooth the skin back
in place. Heat a little olive oil in a non-
stick pan and cook the chicken on
a medium heat for 7–8 minutes on each
side. Remove from the pan.

■ Pull the leaves off the remaining
thyme stalks. Add the thyme, lemon
juice, zest and some seasoning to the
pasta and toss well. Add the white wine
to the chicken pan and bring to the boil,
stirring to incorporate the nice sticky
bits on the bottom. Slice each chicken
breast into 4. Serve the tossed pasta
topped with the chicken and pour over
the juices from the pan. **Serves 4**

Spanish chicken

15 minutes

chicken breasts 2, skin on
chorizo sausage 50g, thinly sliced
cumin seeds 2 tsp
garlic 1 clove, crushed
sherry 2 tbsp
chickpeas 1 tin, about 400g, drained
     and rinsed
tomatoes 2 large, roughly chopped
pepper, salt and chilli sauce to season
coriander leaves to serve

■ Heat a frying pan over a medium heat, add the chicken breasts, skin-side down, and cook for 4 minutes. Turn over and add the chorizo (if the slices are large, cut into 4), the cumin and the garlic. Cook for a further 2 minutes, then splash in the sherry.

■ Allow to bubble for a couple of minutes, then stir in the chickpeas and tomatoes. Season with salt, pepper and chilli sauce and cook for another 2 minutes or until the chicken is cooked through. Serve scattered with coriander leaves. **Serves 2**

You can use chicken thighs for this dish if you prefer; they'll cook in the same time.

Chicken wrapped in Parma ham

45 minutes

chicken fillets 6 skinless
roasted peppers 1 jar or from the deli
    counter (about 440g)
char-grilled aubergines 1 jar or from the
    deli counter (about 200g)
Parma ham 12 slices
rosemary 6 sprigs
baby fennel 6, to serve

Roasted or char-grilled peppers and
aubergines can both be bought in jars,
or by weight from a deli counter.

■ Heat the oven to 180°C/fan 160°C/gas 4.
Put the chicken fillets on a board,
skinned-side down. With a small knife,
make a 'pocket' in the fillet by cutting
along its length; if there is an extra bit of
fillet attached then fold this back and
make your cut under it. Be careful not to
cut all the way through.
■ Fill each pocket with a slice each of
pepper and aubergine. Lay 2 slices of the
Parma ham out flat, slightly overlapping,
and put a sprig of rosemary in the
middle. Put a fillet on top of the
rosemary and wrap it with the ham.
Repeat with the remaining fillets.
■ Lightly oil a baking sheet, put the
chicken on it and cook in the oven for
35 minutes. Serve the fillets whole or,
for a more glam look, cut each one in half
at an angle, and serve drizzled with the
cooking juices. Serve with baby fennel
steamed for about 8 minutes or until
tender. **Serves 6**

Warm chicken and cashew salad

10 minutes

chicken 1 roasted
mixed leaf salad 1 bag (choose one with
    red leaves)
pear 1 large, quartered and core removed
honey-roasted cashews (or other
    sweetened nuts such as pecans) 100g

DRESSING
red wine vinegar 2 tbsp
walnut oil 5 tbsp
Dijon mustard ½ tsp
spring onions 4, sliced

■ Remove the meat from the chicken, discarding most of the skin and all of the bones. Pile the salad leaves on 4 plates and slice a pear quarter over each one. Sprinkle over the nuts.
■ Pour the vinegar, oil, mustard and some seasoning into a small jar and shake well. Add the spring onions and shake again. Arrange the chicken on the salads and pour over the dressing.
Serves 4

Another well-flavoured nut oil, such as hazelnut, can be used instead of walnut.

Chinese poached chicken with dipping sauce

15 minutes

chicken breasts 2 skinless

ketchap manis (Indonesian sweet soy sauce; available at Waitrose and Sainsbury's) 4 tbsp

red chilli ½ thumb-size, seeded and chopped

garlic 1 clove, finely chopped

ginger 1 tsp, finely chopped

lime 1 large, juiced

cucumber 1 medium, shaved into ribbons with a peeler

coriander leaves a small handful, roughly chopped

spring onions 2 green or purple, finely sliced

■ Bring a large saucepan of salted water to the boil and add the chicken breasts. Turn off the heat, cover and leave for 15 minutes. Mix the ketchap manis, red chilli, garlic, ginger and lime juice. Lift the chicken from the water and thinly slice. Serve the chicken, along with the sauce, on top of the cucumber. Sprinkle the coriander and spring onion over the chicken. **Serves 2**

Ketchap manis can be substituted with 4 tbsp soy sauce and 2 tsp honey.

Lemony chicken kebabs

30 minutes

chicken breasts 2, or thighs 4, skinless,
    cut into cubes
garlic 1 clove, crushed
olive oil
lemons 5, 4 quartered and 1 juiced
red pepper 1, cut into squares
bay leaves 8–12
salad leaves to serve

■ Mix the chicken with the garlic, a slosh
of oil and the lemon juice. Thread on to
4 metal skewers, alternating with lemon
quarters, red pepper and bay leaves.
Season well. Barbecue, griddle (char-grill)
or grill on both sides for about 4 minutes
or until the chicken is cooked through.
Serve with salad leaves. **Serves 2**

Metal skewers work well for all methods
of cooking as they won't burn. If you use
bamboo ones, make sure you soak them
thoroughly first.

Turkey and tarragon pot pies

50 minutes

onion 1, halved and sliced
chestnut mushrooms 100g, quartered
butter for frying
cooked turkey or chicken 400g, torn
    into chunks
frozen peas 100g, defrosted
chicken stock fresh, cube or concentrate,
    made up to 300ml
tarragon small bunch, leaves chopped
double cream 142ml carton
puff pastry 2 sheets of fresh or frozen
    ready-rolled, cut to fit 4 pie dishes
egg 1, beaten for glazing

■ Heat the oven to 200°C/fan 180°C/gas 6. Cook the onion and mushrooms in a little butter until soft, add the rest of the ingredients (except the pastry and egg), bubble everything together until a creamy sauce forms and season.
■ Divide among 4 small, ovenproof pie dishes, cover each with a circle of puff pastry, wetting the rims so the pastry sticks, and glaze with egg. Bake for 20–25 minutes until the pastry is puffed and golden. **Serves 4**

Puff pastry made with butter has a superior taste, but you can add flavour to ordinary puff pastry by brushing it with melted butter before glazing with egg.

Easy mouclade

20 minutes

---

mussels 1kg
white wine 125ml
shallots 3, finely sliced
egg yolks 2
double cream 142ml carton
curry powder 1 tsp
lemon 1

You can buy ready-scrubbed mussels in most major supermarkets in 1 kg bags and slightly wilder-looking ones at fishmongers.

■ Rinse the mussels and throw away any that won't close when tapped on the sink. Put them in a large saucepan with the wine and shallots, bring to the boil, cover and steam for 3–4 minutes. Shake the pan from time to time until the mussels have all opened; throw away any that are still closed. Pour through a sieve, reserving the cooking liquid.

■ Mix the egg yolks with the cream and curry powder. Whisk this into the cooking liquid and reheat it gently without letting it boil. Season well with salt, pepper and a squeeze of lemon. Divide the mussels among four bowls and pour over the sauce. Serve with bread to mop up the juices. **Serves 4**

Grilled mackerel with herbed bulgar wheat

30 minutes

bulgar wheat 200g
lemons 2, zest and juice
extra-virgin olive oil
flat-leaf parsley a handful, chopped
mint a handful, chopped
rocket a handful, chopped
cucumber ½, peeled and finely chopped
mackerel fillets 4–8, depending on size
limes 2, halved to serve

■ Put the bulgar wheat in a bowl, cover with boiling water and soak for about 20 minutes or until softened. Drain well, then tip into a large bowl.

■ Combine the lemon zest, juice and 3 tbsp oil. Add to the bowl with the herbs, rocket and cucumber. Mix well, then season to taste. Brush the skin of the mackerel fillets with a little oil and season both sides. Put, skin-side up, under a hot grill for 4–5 minutes until cooked.

■ To serve, spoon a large pile of herbed bulgar wheat on to a serving plate and set the fillets on top. Serve with lime halves for squeezing over. **Serves 4**

You could also use red mullet fillets or even whole sardines for this recipe.

Char-grilled tuna and green beans with salsa verde

15 minutes

green beans 300g, trimmed
cherry tomatoes 200g, halved
tuna steaks 4
tarragon leaves chopped, 2 tbsp

SALSA VERDE
parsley a small bunch
basil a small bunch
anchovy fillets 4
capers 2 tbsp, rinsed and drained
garlic 1 clove
lemon 1, juiced
olive oil

■ Make the salsa verde by whizzing the parsley, basil, anchovy fillets, capers, garlic, lemon and 150ml olive oil in a food processor. Season.

■ Cook the beans until tender then toss with a couple of tablespoons of salsa verde and the tomatoes. Griddle (char-grill) the tuna for 2–3 minutes each side. Serve on a bed of dressed beans with a drizzle of extra salsa verde and the tarragon sprinkled over. **Serves 4**

When buying tuna, look for a deep, dark-red colour and no obvious fishy smell.

Fennel and prawns with orecchiette

15 minutes

orecchiette 400g
olive oil
large raw and peeled prawns 250g
garlic 1 large clove, finely chopped
fennel 1 large or 3 small bulbs, thinly
    sliced
watercress a couple of handfuls
chives 2 tbsp, finely chopped
lemons 2, juiced

■ Cook the pasta in boiling water following the pack instructions. Drain. Heat a couple of tbsp olive oil in a frying pan and add the prawns and garlic. Fry for two minutes until the prawns are pink and cooked through. Add the fennel and watercress, and toss until just wilted.
■ Take off the heat and stir through the chives and lemon juice. Season well. Serve dressed with a little more olive oil.
Serves 4

If you want to make this dish look even smarter, use linguine instead of orecchiette.

Red mullet and purple-sprouting broccoli with capers and anchovies

20 minutes

---

butter 1 tbsp
anchovy fillets 4
garlic 1 clove, crushed
red mullet 4 fillets
purple-sprouting broccoli 200g
capers 1 tbsp, rinsed and drained

■ Melt butter in a pan and heat until foaming. Add the anchovies and garlic and stir until melted. Splash in 4 tbsp water and whisk to make a sauce. Remove from the heat and brush a little over the fillets and put them, skin-side-up, on an oiled baking sheet. Grill the fillets for around 2 minutes on each side.

■ Cutting any very fat stems in half lengthways, steam the broccoli for 3–4 minutes until tender. Divide between two warmed plates, Reheat the sauce with a little more water if necessary and stir in the capers. Spoon most of it over the broccoli, top with the fish and the last of the sauce. **Serves 2**

Anchovy fillets come in both oil and salt; the salted ones need a good rinse before use.

Seared salmon with quick hollandaise

20 minutes

asparagus 8 spears, ends trimmed
broad beans 2 handfuls
olive oil
salmon fillets 2

SAUCE
egg yolks 2
butter 50g, melted
lemon 1, juiced
tarragon and basil a handful of each,
    chopped

■ Put the eggs in a blender and, with the motor running, pour in the hot butter until the mixture thickens. Season with lemon juice, salt and pepper. Stir in the herbs.

■ Meanwhile, cook the asparagus and broad beans separately in boiling water for 2–3 minutes until just cooked through. Pop the broad beans out of their skins if you prefer (they can be a bit tough). Heat a little oil in a frying pan and cook the salmon skin-side down for 2 minutes, then turn over and cook for 4 minutes, or until cooked through. Serve the salmon with the vegetables and hollandaise. **Serves 2**

If your hollandaise doesn't thicken first time, start with a new egg yolk in the blender and add the mixture in a thin stream with the motor running.

Trout with brown butter and almonds

15 minutes

butter 50g
trout fillets 4 small, skin on
flaked almonds a handful, lightly toasted
lemon juice of ½
mixed herbs (such as parsley, thyme and chives), leaves finely chopped, 3 tbsp
new potatoes and asparagus steamed, to serve

■ Heat the butter in a frying pan until it begins to turn nutty brown, add the trout fillets, skin-side down, and cook for 3 minutes each side or until cooked through. Lift on to 2 serving plates. Add the almonds to the pan with a squeeze of lemon juice, some seasoning and the herbs. Swirl to mix everything then pour over the fillets. Serve with the new potatoes and asparagus. **Serves 2**

Most bought trout is of the farmed, rainbow variety – look out for organic or sustainably grown if it is available.

Prawn curry

20 minutes

---

coconut milk 400ml tin
green chillies 3 (the long Indian ones;
    remove the seeds if you don't like
    it too hot)
coriander leaves 1 bunch, chopped
groundnut oil
onion 1, sliced
root ginger 2cm piece, grated
garlic 2 cloves, sliced
garam masala 2 tsp
ground turmeric 1 tsp
large raw and peeled prawns 400g
red chilli to garnish (optional)
lime or lemon wedges to serves

■ Put a little of the coconut milk in a blender with the green chillies and most of the coriander. Whiz to a thin paste, add the rest of the coconut milk and whiz again.

■ Heat a little oil in a saucepan and fry the onion for a minute or 2 until soft. Add the ginger and garlic and fry for another minute. Stir in the garam masala and turmeric and stir again – the mixture should smell very fragrant.

■ Add the coconut mixture and bring to the boil, simmer for 10 minutes, then stir in the prawns and cook for 3 minutes or until they are cooked through. Stir in the rest of the coriander. Top with the red chilli (if using) and serve with basmati rice and lime or lemon wedges. **Serves 4**

If you don't have a blender then chop everything for the coconut mixture as finely as you can and mix it together.

Baked fish in rich tomatoey sauce

45 minutes

plaice or other white fish fillets 4 × 175g,
   skin removed
basil a handful of leaves

SAUCE
onions 2, sliced
olive oil
garlic 4 cloves, sliced
plum tomatoes 2 × 400g tins

■ Heat the oven to 190°C/170°C/gas 5. Put the onions with a little (think tsp not tbsp) olive oil in an ovenproof dish. Cook for 15 minutes until softened and tinged with brown. Stir in the garlic, tomatoes and some seasoning and return to the oven for another 15 minutes. Sit the fish on top of the sauce, season and bake for a final 10–15 minutes. Tear over the basil and serve. **Serves 4**

You can make the tomato base ahead if you want to save time. Warm it up though, before you cook the fish.

Clams with linguine

15 minutes

clams in their shells, 450g
linguine 400g
olive oil
streaky bacon 6 rashers, chopped
shallots 4, finely chopped
garlic 2 cloves, crushed
sherry 250ml
flat-leaf parsley a large handful, finely
    chopped

Clams need to be live when you cook
them. Check by making sure they will
close when raw by tapping them.

■ Rinse the clams in cold water and
throw away any that are broken or won't
close when tapped on the sink. Drain.
Cook the linguine following the packet
instructions.

■ Put 4 tbsp olive oil in a large saucepan
and fry the bacon until crisp. Add the
shallots and garlic and fry for 1–2
minutes until the shallots are soft.
Add the sherry and clams and put a lid
on the pan. Cook, shaking the pan until
all the clams have opened – about
3 minutes (throw away any that won't).
Add the parsley.

■ Drain the linguine and tip it into a
large bowl, pour the clam mixture over
the top, season with salt and freshly
milled black pepper and toss together.
Serves 4

Easy smoked salmon and thyme risotto

25 minutes

butter 50g
shallots 2, finely chopped
garlic 2 cloves, finely chopped
risotto rice 250g
thyme or lemon thyme leaves, 1 tbsp
chicken or vegetable stock fresh, cube or
    concentrate, 800ml
white wine 100ml
smoked salmon 400g sliced
Parmesan cheese 2 tbsp, freshly grated
lemon wedges for serving

■ Melt the butter in a pan. Add the shallots, garlic, rice and thyme, and cook for 1 minute. Stir in the stock and white wine. Cover and cook, stirring over a low heat for 15 minutes until the liquid is absorbed and the rice is just *al dente*. Cut half the salmon slices into fine ribbons and leave the remainder whole. Stir the salmon ribbons and Parmesan into the rice mixture. Season. Spoon into bowls and add the salmon slices. Serve with lemon wedges. **Serves 4**

Smoked salmon varies in texture and depth of flavour. Choose one you like to eat on its own, even though you are going to cook it.

Thai red curry

20 minutes

vegetable or sunflower oil 2 tbsp
red curry paste 2–3 tbsp
coconut milk 400g tin
butternut squash ½, cut into chunks
baby corn 8, halved
large peeled prawns 24
mangetout 2 handfuls, sliced in half
    lengthways

■ Heat the oil in a large wok or frying pan, fry the paste for a few minutes until it becomes fragrant, then add the coconut milk. Bring to the boil, then add the corn and squash. Cook for 5 minutes, or until the squash is tender, then add the prawns and mangetout and cook for 3 minutes until cooked through. Serve with rice. **Serves 4**

You can vary the veg in this: baby potatoes, cherry tomatoes, green beans and broccoli all work well.

Salmon teriyaki salad

20 minutes

soy sauce 5 tbsp
rice wine vinegar (from supermarkets) or
    dry sherry 5 tbsp
dark brown sugar 2 tbsp
salmon fillets 4
oil
rice noodles 250g, cooked following
    packet instructions
red chilli 1, chopped
spring onions 1 bunch, chopped
baby leaf spinach 100g
coriander leaves a small bunch, chopped
sesame seeds 1 tbsp, toasted
sesame oil 2 tsp, to serve

■ Heat the soy, vinegar and sugar in a pan until the sugar dissolves. Pour over the salmon and marinate for 5 minutes.
■ Heat the oil in a pan, add the salmon and cook, skin-side down, for 5 minutes until crisp, then turn and cook for 3 minutes. Add the marinade and simmer for a few minutes until reduced and sticky. Mix the noodles with the rest of the ingredients (except the sesame oil). Serve with the salmon and drizzle with the sesame oil. **Serves 4**

Rice noodles come in varying widths; you can use fat ones, as in the picture, or thin vermicelli if you prefer.

Asian-style brill with greens

20 minutes

---

brill steaks or fillets 4, about 175g each

garlic 2 cloves, finely diced

ginger 5cm piece, finely diced

vegetable oil

tamarind paste 2 tsp

soy sauce 2 tbsp

red or yellow chillies 2 small, deseeded
and finely sliced

coriander leaves 1 bunch, roughly
chopped, with a few leaves reserved
for garnish

greens 400g (red chard and spring
greens are good), ends trimmed
and left in large pieces

spring onions 2, shredded

■ Heat the oven to 200°C/fan 180°C/gas 6. Score one side of the brill steaks (or the skin-side of the fillets) with a sharp knife and rub with the garlic and ginger. Lightly drizzle a baking tray with oil and add the fish (if using fillets, place skin-side up). Roast for 8 minutes (6 minutes for fillets).

■ In a small pan, mix the tamarind paste with 75ml hot water until smooth. Add the soy sauce and half the chillies and gently warm. Remove from the heat and stir in most of the chopped coriander.

■ Steam the greens for 2–4 minutes until tender. Transfer to plates and top with the roast brill. Scatter with the spring onions, remaining chillies and coriander leaves, and serve with the tamarind sauce. **Serves 4**

Tamarind paste or purée is sold in jars; you'll usually find it with the spices.

Prawn, mango and spinach salad

15 minutes

---

young spinach leaves ½ of a 225g bag
cooked and peeled tiger prawns 200g
mango 1 large, peeled and thinly sliced
shallot 1 **or spring onions** 2, sliced
    very thinly

DRESSING
root ginger 2cm piece, grated or finely
    chopped
dry sherry 1 tbsp
orange ½, zested and juiced
sunflower oil 3 tbsp
toasted sesame oil 1 tsp

■ Make the dressing by whisking the ginger, sherry, orange zest and juice and oils in a bowl. Season lightly. You can do this in advance if it suits.

■ When ready to serve, lay the spinach in a bowl and top with the prawns and mango. Pour over the dressing and fold together gently. Sprinkle the shallot or spring onion on top. **Serves 4**

If you end up buying a new bottle of sherry for the dressing, then choose a good one and also serve with the meal.

Crisp sea bass with Vietnamese vegetables

40 minutes

vegetable oil 4 tbsp

root ginger finger-length piece, cut into matchsticks

garlic 2 cloves, crushed

red chillies 2, finely chopped

lemongrass 1, finely sliced

sea bass fillets 6 large or 12 small (1kg in total), descaled

small leeks 200g, sliced diagonally

baby corn 200g, trimmed

bok choi 200g, cut in wedges

spring onions 6, sliced

light soy sauce 2 tbsp

■ Heat 2 tbsp of the vegetable oil in a wok and cook the ginger, garlic, chillies and lemongrass for 5 minutes over a low heat. Set aside.

■ Heat another 2 tbsp oil in a large non-stick frying pan and cook the sea bass skin-side down in batches for 4 minutes. Carefully turn over and cook on the other side for 1 minute. Keep warm.

■ Reheat the ginger mixture in the wok until sizzling. Stir in the vegetables and cook over a medium heat for about 5 minutes until tender. Add the soy sauce and toss. Serve the sea bass on a pile of vegetables. **Serves 6**

If you want to be flash with your sea bass, make a series of little cuts along the length of the fillet through the skin, before cooking.

Warm crab noodle salad

15 minutes

rice vermicelli noodles 100g
limes 3, juiced
fish sauce 1 tsp
light muscovado sugar 1 tbsp
sweet chilli dipping sauce 1 tbsp
root ginger 1 tbsp, freshly grated
red onion ½, thinly sliced
white crab meat 170g, drained well
sugar snaps or mangetout a handful,
    halved lengthways
fresh coriander leaves a good handful,
    roughly chopped
lime wedges to serve

■ Soak the noodles in boiling water for 3 minutes or until softened. Drain well and put in a medium bowl. You may want to cut them into shorter pieces with scissors so that they mix with the other ingredients more easily. Put the lime juice, fish sauce, sugar, dipping sauce and ginger in a small glass jar and shake well. Toss the onion, crab, sugar snaps and coriander through the noodles. Pour the dressing over, toss and serve with lime wedges. **Serves 2**

You can buy fresh or frozen crab meat from fish counters and fishmongers, or you can use tinned if it's easier.

Smoked trout on gremolata cannellini beans

10 minutes

cannellini beans 400g can, drained
red onion ½, finely chopped
lemon 1
flat-leaf parsley a handful of leaves,
    roughly chopped
garlic 1 clove, crushed
extra-virgin olive oil
smoked trout fillets 2 (about 100g)

■ Rinse the beans with boiling water and put them in a medium bowl. Add the onion. Grate the zest from half the lemon. Halve the lemon and squeeze the juice from the zested half. Cut the other half into wedges. Mix the parsley, garlic, lemon juice and 3 tbsp olive oil. Season well and mix half into the beans.

■ Divide between 2 plates and put the trout on top. Serve with lemon wedges and the remaining dressing. **Serves 2**

If you can't get smoked trout, try this with smoked mackerel or even smoked salmon.

Hot-smoked salmon with couscous and roast vegetables

40 minutes

red onions 2, cut into wedges

courgettes 2, chopped

red peppers 2, chopped

olive oil

sea salt and freshly ground black pepper
to season

couscous 150g

vegetable or chicken stock powder or
cube, made up to 300ml

lemon 1, zest and juice

soured cream 142ml carton

flat-leaf parsley a small bunch, chopped

hot-smoked salmon 200g, flaked into
large chunks

■ Heat the oven to 200°C/fan 180°C/gas 6. Put the onions, courgettes and red peppers in a large roasting tray, drizzle with 2 tbsp olive oil, season with sea salt and freshly ground black pepper and toss well to coat. Roast for 20 minutes until browned and cooked.

■ Meanwhile, put the couscous in a bowl, add the hot stock, lemon zest and juice and some seasoning. Mix well and cover tightly with cling film. Leave to swell for 5 minutes. Mix the soured cream and parsley together.

■ To serve, spoon the couscous on to 4 plates and top each with roast vegetables, salmon and a spoonful of the herbed soured cream. **Serves 4**

Most supermarkets stock hot-smoked salmon, though some call it hot-roast or even honey-roast.

Mini Wellingtons

25 minutes

fillet steaks 4, thick cut, brushed with
a little olive oil and seasoned
mushroom pâté 4 tbsp, use a good-
quality bought one
ready-rolled puff pastry 2 × 375g packs,
each cut into 4
egg 1, beaten
green beans steamed, to serve

■ Heat the oven to 220°C/fan 200°C/gas 7.
Char-grill or sear the steaks for 30 seconds
each side. Cool slightly, then top each
with pâté and put them on a piece of
pastry. Lay another piece of pastry on top
and press the edges together firmly. Trim,
leaving a border, and seal. Glaze with egg,
then bake for 12 minutes for medium
rare. Serve with the green beans. **Serves 4**

When cooking steaks, oil the meat rather
than the pan to stop it sticking.

Peppered sirloin steak with watercress salad

15 minutes

olive oil

sirloin steaks 4, about 175g each

sea salt and freshly ground black pepper
to season

watercress a large bunch, roughly
shredded

radishes 2 bunches, roughly chopped

balsamic vinegar 3 tbsp

■ Heat a griddle or frying pan until really hot. Rub some olive oil on each side of the steaks and sprinkle generously with freshly ground black pepper. Press the pepper on firmly. Cook the steaks on each side: 2–3 minute for rare, 4 minutes for medium rare and 6 minutes for well done.

■ Mix the shredded watercress and chopped radishes in a bowl with 4 tbsp olive oil and the balsamic vinegar. Serve each steak topped with a generous handful of salad and a sprinkle of sea salt. **Serves 4**

Serve this with boiled or steamed potatoes if you are feeling good, or chips if you are feeling bad.

Sticky gammon steaks

15 minutes

Chinese five-spice powder 1 tsp
gammon steaks 2
olive oil
red chilli 1, finely chopped
orange 1, zested and juiced
clear honey 2 tbsp
soy sauce 1 tbsp

■ Sprinkle the five-spice powder over the gammon steaks. Heat 2 tbsp oil in a large frying pan and cook over a high heat for 2 minutes until the edges are tinged brown. Add the chilli, orange zest and juice, honey and soy sauce, and simmer rapidly until the sauce is sticky and the gammon is glazed and golden with almost burnt edges. Serve immediately with steamed greens and rice, and with any pan juices poured over. **Serves 2**

This recipe also works well with pork steaks or chops.

Lamb fillet with asparagus and sugar snaps

30 minutes

---

lamb neck fillet 300g
lamb seasoning 2 tsp ready mixed, or
    make your own with 1 tsp dried
    oregano, 1 tsp paprika, salt and pepper
asparagus 1 bunch, trimmed
sugar snaps 150g, trimmed
butter
lemon ½, juiced

■ Rub the lamb all over with seasoning, then grill: 15 minutes for rare and 25 minutes for medium. Turn the lamb as it cooks so that it evenly browns. When cooked, allow to rest for 5 minutes. Cook the asparagus and sugar snaps in boiling water for 2 minutes, drain well and toss in a knob of butter with the lemon juice and some seasoning. Slice the lamb and serve with the lemony vegetables.
Serves 2

This lamb recipe works very well on a barbecue; it will still take only 30 minutes.

Chorizo toad-in-the-hole with roast onions

30 minutes

chorizo sausages 8 small or 4 large
shallots or baby onions 6, peeled
flour 125g
eggs 3
milk 300ml
rosemary 4 sprigs

Any type of sausage will work equally well for this dish.

■ Heat the oven to 200°C/fan 180°C/gas 6. Roast the sausages and the shallots in an ovenproof dish, about 25×30cm, or 4 individual dishes, for 10 minutes.

■ Put the flour, eggs, milk and a pinch of salt in a jug and, using a hand-held blender or mixer, whiz until smooth. Add the rosemary to the sausages then pour in the batter. Increase the oven heat to 220°C/gas 200°C/gas 7 and cook for 20 minutes until puffed up and golden.

Serves 4

Lemon and spice-rub steak

30 minutes

___

ready-prepared potato wedges 500g
olive oil
smoked paprika 1 tsp
lemon 1, grated zest and juice (juice for
    the dressing)
ground cumin ½ tsp
sirloin steaks 4 × 175g
Greek yoghurt 150g
mint a small bunch, roughly chopped
watercress 125g pack, straggly stalks
    pulled off
fennel bulb 1 bulb, sliced finely
cucumber 1, deseeded and chopped
lime 1, juiced

■ Heat the oven to 220°C/fan 200°C/gas 7. Tip the potato wedges into a roasting tin and toss with 2 tbsp of the olive oil. Roast for 25 minutes.

■ Meanwhile, mix the paprika, lemon zest and cumin with a further 2 tbsp olive oil and brush over both sides of the steaks.

■ For the dressing, mix the yoghurt with the lemon juice and chopped mint, and season. For the salad, toss together the watercress leaves, fennel and cucumber with 2 tbsp olive oil and the lime juice. Season.

■ Heat a griddle pan until very hot and cook each steak for about 3–4 minutes each side for medium rare and a few minutes longer for well done. Serve the steaks with the roasted potato wedges, salad and good dollop of yoghurt dressing. **Serves 4**

You can use raw potatoes rather than ready-made wedges, but you'll have to cut them thinly so they cook in time.

Pork fillet with mustard-seed Puy lentils

45 minutes

olive oil

pork fillet 300g, trimmed

wholegrain mustard 2 tbsp

Puy lentils 200g

potatoes 100g, cut into chunks

red onions 2 small, peeled and quartered

sun-dried tomatoes in olive oil 6, drained

thyme 2 decent-size sprigs

beef stock powder or cube, made up
    to 700ml

flat-leaf parsley 3 tbsp, chopped

■ Heat a little olive oil in a deep frying pan, season the pork and spread with half of the mustard. Fry for a couple of minutes until lightly browned all over. Remove the pork from the pan and set aside.

■ Add the lentils, potatoes, onions, sun-dried tomatoes and thyme to the frying pan. Then mix the remaining mustard into the stock, pour over the lentil mixture and cook for 15 minutes.

■ Top with the pork fillet, cover and cook for a further 15 minutes.

■ Leave the fillet to rest for 5 minutes before carving. Stir the parsley into the lentil mixture and serve with slices of pork. **Serves 2**

This recipe easily doubles to serve 4 for a dinner party.

Béarnaise butter steaks

15 minutes

butter 250g, softened

shallot 1, finely chopped

white wine vinegar 2 tsp

fresh tarragon a small handful, roughly
chopped

sirloin steaks 2, brushed with a little oil
and seasoned

mixed salad leaves 2 handfuls, to serve

■ Mash the butter, shallot, vinegar and
tarragon together. Roll into a sausage,
wrap in cling film and freeze until firm.
Sear the steaks in a very hot pan for
2 minutes on each side for rare (3 for
medium), cover and rest for 2 minutes.
Top each steak with a slice of the butter.
(Freeze the remaining butter to use
later.) Serve with some salad leaves.
Serves 2

To time steaks accurately, bring them
to room temperature first.

Calf's liver with red wine, onions and sage

30 minutes

potatoes 600g
butter 100g
spring onions 5, finely sliced
sage a bunch, finely chopped
olive oil
calf's liver 4 slices (each about 140g)
red wine 1 glass

Calf's liver is milder in taste than some livers, but you could use other types.

■ Simmer the potatoes in water for 20 minutes. Drain the potatoes and crush, adding half the butter, the spring onions and sage. Season to taste.

■ Meanwhile, heat a knob of butter and 1 tbsp olive oil in a frying pan and fry the liver for 4 minutes on each side. Remove from the pan and keep warm.

■ Add the red wine and remaining butter to the pan in which the liver was cooked and boil rapidly for 4 minutes. Put some mash on each plate, top with the liver and spoon over the red wine sauce.

Serves 4

Sausages braised with Guinness and onions

1 hour

pork sausages 8, large fat ones
olive oil
onions 2, sliced
streaky bacon 4–6 rashers, chopped
garlic 1 clove, crushed
plain flour 2 tsp
Guinness 330ml can
thyme 2 sprigs
mashed potato made with lots of cream
    and butter, to serve

■ Heat the oven to 180°C/fan 160°C/gas 4. Brown the sausage with a little olive oil in an ovenproof dish. Throw in the onions, cook until soft, then add the bacon and garlic and cook for 2 minutes. Stir in the flour, pour the Guinness over, let it bubble, then add the thyme. Cover and bake for 40 minutes. Serve with mash. **Serves 4**

The sausage is the star here, so treat everyone to the best-quality banger you can afford.

Chilli-lemon lamb cutlets

15 minutes

lamb cutlets 6
lemon 1, halved
natural yoghurt 2 tbsp
Tabasco sauce a few dashes
turmeric ½ tsp
garlic 1 clove, crushed
coriander leaves chopped, 2 tbsp
naan bread or rice to serve

■ Put the lamb cutlets in a bowl and squeeze one of the lemon halves over them. Add the rest of the ingredients and rub everything into the lamb well.

■ Heat the grill to high, then grill the cutlets for 2 minutes on each side. Squeeze over the remaining lemon half. Serve with naan bread or rice and more yoghurt if you like. **Serves 2**

If you prefer, use a curry powder instead of turmeric.

Warm steak and blue cheese salad

15 minutes

sirloin steaks 2, fat removed
red wine vinegar 2 tbsp good quality
Dijon mustard 1 tsp
olive oil
salad leaves 2 handfuls
Gorgonzola or creamy blue cheese 100g,
   crumbled

■ Heat a griddle (char-grill) or frying pan to very hot. Oil and season the steaks, then cook for 2 minutes each side for rare, 3 for medium. Rest for 5 minutes under foil. Whisk the vinegar and mustard with 4 tbsp oil. Slice the steak and toss with the salad and dressing. Top with the cheese. **Serves 2**

Look out for Forum Cabernet Sauvignon red wine vinegar – it will give your dressing extra depth.

Cider-cured pork chops with apple and rocket salad

30 minutes

cider 1 × 500ml bottle (dry or sweet but
    make it good quality)
rock salt 3 tbsp
light muscovado sugar 4 tbsp
bay leaves 2
cinnamon sticks 2
pork chops 4, fat trimmed if you prefer
garlic 2 cloves, crushed
shallot 1, finely chopped
eating apples 2
cider vinegar and olive oil to dress
rocket and watercress 2 handfuls

■ Bring the cider, salt, sugar, bay leaves and cinnamon sticks to a slow boil in a saucepan. Put the pork chops in a ceramic dish with the garlic and shallot and pour over the cider mixture, leave for 10 minutes.

■ Take the chops out of the marinade and pat dry. Season well with black pepper and grill on each side for 7–10 minutes until browned and cooked through. Make sure you cook the fat through properly.

■ Meanwhile, slice the apples thinly and toss them in a splash of cider vinegar, put in a bowl with the rocket and watercress and dress with olive oil and more vinegar if you need to. Season well. **Serves 4**

If you want to leave this to marinade for longer, you must cool the liquid down first.

Venison sausages with polenta

30 minutes

olive oil
venison sausages 6 (available in most supermarkets)
onion 1, thickly sliced
red wine 100ml
passata 500ml
black olives 8, stoned
quick-cook polenta 150g
vegetable stock granules (such as Marigold) 1 tbsp, or cube 1, crumbled
butter 25g
flat-leaf parsley chopped, 2 tbsp

■ Heat 1 tbsp olive oil in a large frying pan. Add the sausages and onion and fry for 10 minutes, turning occasionally, until the sausages are browned. Pour in the wine, let it bubble for a few seconds, then stir in the passata and olives. Cook gently for 10–15 minutes, adding a little water if it gets too dry.

■ Meanwhile, put the polenta in a saucepan with 1 litre water and the stock granules or crumbled cube. Bring to the boil, stirring often, then simmer for 5 minutes (continue stirring) until it is thick and creamy. Stir in the butter. Serve topped with the sausage and onion sauce with the parsley scattered over.

Serves 2 generously

Use quick-cook polenta, so it's ready to serve in 10 minutes.

Parmesan and tapenade-crusted lamb cutlets with crushed potatoes and peas

30 minutes

---

new potatoes 300g
frozen petit pois 150g
lamb cutlets 6 (or 4 chops)
black olive tapenade for spreading
Parmesan cheese grated, 4–6 tbsp
butter 50g
mint 1 bunch, chopped

■ Simmer the potatoes for about 18 minutes until cooked. Add the petit pois and cook for a further 2 minutes.

■ Cook the lamb under a hot grill for 4 minutes. Remove from the heat and turn over. Spread the uncooked sides with a little tapenade, top with the Parmesan and return to the grill for a further 6 minutes, until bubbling.

■ Drain the cooked potatoes and peas, add the butter, season with salt and pepper and roughly crush with a wooden spoon or masher. Stir in the mint and serve with the lamb cutlets. **Serves 2**

Tapenade is available made with black or green olives. Choose the one you like best.

Beef, radish and pea salad

20 minutes

peas in the pod 500g or **frozen peas** 250g
fillet steak 1 × 200g piece
black peppercorns 1 tbsp, crushed
radishes 150g
half-fat crème fraîche 200ml
cress, or mustard and cress 1 box
lime 1, cut into wedges

Resting the steak stops all the juices running out of it as soon as you cut it.

■ Shell the peas and cook them briefly in well-salted boiling water until just tender (1–2 minutes). Drain and cook under running cold water.

■ Roll the beef in the crushed peppercorns. Heat a frying pan until very hot and cook the beef for about 2 minutes on each side (less if the steak is thin). Rest for 5 minutes. Slice the radishes and pile on a serving plate. Scatter over the peas. Slice the beef thinly and arrange over the top. Thin the crème fraîche with 2–3 tsp water if necessary and trickle over the top of the beef. Snip the cress over the plate. Serve with the lime.

Serves 2 as a main, **4** as a starter

Pork chops with cider, cream and spinach

30 minutes

olive oil
pork chops 2, rind snipped off
onion 1, sliced
cider 200ml
double cream 142ml carton
wholegrain or Dijon mustard 1 tbsp
spinach 100g
butter

■ Heat the oil in a frying pan, season the chops then fry until browned. Remove, add the onion and cook for about 10 minutes until soft and caramelised. Add the cider, bring to a bubble and reduce a little. Add the cream and mustard, stir, bring to a simmer then put the chops back in and cook for 8–10 minutes or until cooked through.

■ Meanwhile, cook the spinach in a large pan or wok with a knob of butter and some seasoning until wilted. Serve the chops and sauce with the spinach.

Serves 2

Buy the best-quality pork you can; well-farmed pork has an appreciably better texture and flavour.

Lemon lamb cutlets with Greek salad

25 minutes

lemon 1, zested and juiced
dried oregano 1 tsp
garlic 1 fat clove, crushed
olive oil
lamb cutlets 6 small
cherry tomatoes a handful, halved
cucumber ¼, diced
feta cheese 50g, cubed
mixed olives in olive oil 2 tbsp
baby spinach a handful of leaves, to serve

■ Heat the grill. Mix together the lemon zest, oregano, garlic and 1 tbsp of olive oil. Season the mix, then rub over the lamb cutlets and set aside for 5 minutes.
■ Lightly toss the cherry tomatoes, cucumber, feta and olives with 1 tbsp lemon juice and 2 tbsp of olive oil. Grill the lamb cutlets for 2–3 minutes each side. Serve hot with the Greek salad and some baby spinach. **Serves 2**

Ask your butcher for French-trimmed cutlets for a smarter-looking dish.

Steak with tomato and chilli salad

15 minutes

olive oil
rib-eye steaks 2 × 200g
baby spinach 100g
beef tomato 1 ripe, halved and sliced
chilli ½, finely chopped
feta cheese 100g, crumbled
balsamic vinegar

■ Heat a heavy-based pan, add a little olive oil and fry the steaks on each side: 3 minutes for rare, 4 for medium. Rest, covered, for 10 minutes. Toss the spinach in a bowl with the tomato, chilli and cheese, and dress with olive oil, balsamic and seasoning. Serve with the steak.

Serves 2

If you use a different cut of steak, such as fillet or sirloin, you'll have to adjust the timings depending on how thick they are.

English field mushroom risotto

30 minutes

vegetable stock fresh, cube or powder, made up to 1 litre, heated and kept simmering in a pan

butter 125g

olive oil

garlic 1 clove, crushed

onion 1, finely diced

field mushrooms 200g, sliced

risotto rice such as carnaroli, 300g

white wine 75ml

chives 1 tbsp, chopped

Parmesan cheese 125g, freshly grated to serve

truffle oil to serve (optional)

■ Bring the stock to a gentle simmer. In a pan, melt half of the butter with 1 tbsp olive oil. Add the garlic and onion and fry over a low heat for 3 minutes. Add the mushrooms and cook for a further 3 minutes.

■ Add the rice and stir well, coating each grain with butter and oil. Add enough stock just to cover the rice and simmer gently, stirring frequently until the stock is absorbed. Continue stirring and adding the hot stock, waiting until each batch is absorbed before adding the next. The risotto is ready when the rice is creamy and cooked. Finally, add the wine and stir in the remaining butter and season to taste. Mix well and serve topped with chives, Parmesan and truffle oil, if you like. **Serves 4**

Field mushrooms will turn the risotto quite dark. If you'd like it lighter, use button mushrooms.

Pasta with pesto

30 minutes

baby plum or cherry tomatoes 500g,
   halved
extra-virgin olive oil
balsamic vinegar 1 tbsp
spaghetti 500g
pesto 6–8 tbsp
rocket 2 handfuls

■ Heat the oven to 190°C/fan 170°C/gas 5.
Put the tomatoes on a lined baking sheet.
Drizzle with 2 tbsp olive oil and vinegar.
Season. Roast for about 20 minutes.
■ Cook the pasta following packet
instructions. Drain and mix with the
pesto and rocket. Serve immediately with
the tomatoes scattered over. **Serves 4**

Don't feel guilty buying pesto – choose
a good-quality brand (or try a deli that
makes it fresh), and no one will be any
the wiser.

Pizza Puttanesca

Takes 20 minutes

pizza bases 2, ready made
tomato and chilli sauce or tomato sauce
8 tbsp, good quality from a jar
garlic 1 clove, sliced
anchovies 6, in olive oil, drained
Sunblush or semi-dried tomatoes 100g,
drained
basil leaves a small handful
chilli oil to serve (optional)

■ Heat the oven to 220°C/fan 200°C/
gas 7. Put the pizza bases on 2 baking
trays and spread with the sauce. Scatter
with the garlic, anchovies, olives, capers
and tomatoes.

■ Bake for 10 minutes or until the base is
cooked. Scatter with the fresh basil and
drizzle with some chilli oil, if you like.

Serves 2

Chilli oil is quite potent but does vary in
strength so taste it before you use it too
liberally.

Courgette fritters with tomato and feta salsa

25 minutes

courgettes 3 medium, grated
red onion ½, peeled and finely chopped
cumin seeds 1 tsp
red chilli 1 large, finely chopped
self-raising flour 125g
eggs 2
olive oil for frying

SALSA
cherry tomatoes 125g, quartered
feta cheese 100g, crumbled
mint leaves a handful
lemon ½, juiced

■ Mix the courgette, onion, spices, flour and egg together. Season. Heat 1 tbsp oil in a non-stick frying pan, drop in heaped tbsps of batter. Cook, in batches, for 2–3 minutes each side or until golden and cooked through.

■ Meanwhile mix together the cherry tomatoes, feta, mint and lemon juice, and season. Serve the fritters with the tomato and feta salsa. **Serves 4**

When buying, choose firm courgettes without wrinkles or blemishes, so they grate easily.

Pea and mint risotto

30 minutes

olive oil

butter

onion 1, finely chopped

garlic 2 cloves, finely chopped

risotto rice 400g

white wine 150ml

vegetable stock fresh, cube or powder, made up to 1.5 litres, heated and kept simmering

frozen peas 450g, defrosted

Parmesan cheese 25g, freshly grated

fresh mint a small bunch, chopped

mascarpone 2 tbsp

■ Heat a large, heavy saucepan and add 2 tbsp oil and a knob of butter. When the butter is foaming, add the onion and cook for 5 minutes until beginning to soften. Add the garlic and rice, and cook for a few minutes until the rice is shiny and opaque.

■ Add the wine and boil for 1 minute, stirring constantly. Reduce the heat and add the stock a ladleful at a time, stirring constantly until each ladleful is absorbed, adding the peas with the last ladle. The rice should be creamy but firm to the bite. Remove from heat and stir in the cheese, mint and mascarpone. Season well. **Serves 4**

Try using Grana Padano cheese rather than Parmesan for this recipe. It has a similar texture and flavour.

Warm lemony mushroom salad

15 minutes

olive oil

garlic 2 cloves, crushed

white wine 3 tbsp

lemon 1, juiced

white wine vinegar 1 tsp

golden caster sugar 2 tbsp

chestnut or button mushrooms 250g,
    sliced

baby spinach 200g

red onion 1 small, thinly sliced

walnuts 75g, toasted and roughly
    chopped

Parmesan cheese 60g, roughly grated

■ Heat 5 tbsp olive oil and garlic over a medium heat for 2 minutes. Add the wine, lemon juice, vinegar and sugar, simmer for about 1 minute and then add the sliced mushrooms. Cook until the mushrooms are softened, about 4 minutes.

■ Put the spinach in a big bowl. Scatter the red onion, walnuts and cheese over. Pour the warm mushrooms on top and mix just before serving. **Serves 4**

To lessen the effect of eating raw onion, soak the slices in lemon juice for 10 minutes.

Gnocchi with asparagus

20 minutes

asparagus 1 large bunch, about 250g,
   trimmed
gnocchi 500g
Boursin or other herbed cream cheese
   150g
lemon 1, zested
Parmesan cheese 2 tbsp, freshly grated
parsley 1 tbsp, chopped

You can buy fresh gnocchi from the
chilled cabinets, or a product that doesn't
need chilling from the pasta shelves.

■ Bring 2 pans of salted water to the
boil and heat the grill to its highest
setting. Cut the asparagus into 3–4cm
lengths, keeping the tips separate.
Put the asparagus stems into the boiling
water and cook for 2 minutes, then add
the tips and cook for a further 2 minutes.
Drain thoroughly.
■ Meanwhile, cook the gnocchi in the
other pan: they're ready when they float
to the surface, which only takes a couple
of minutes. Drain the gnocchi.
■ Put the cream cheese in a pan with
8 tbsp water and the lemon zest. Stir
together over a medium heat until the
cheese melts to a creamy sauce. Season
with pepper and a little salt. Stir in the
gnocchi and asparagus, and pile into a
shallow heatproof dish. Scatter over the
Parmesan and parsley and brown under
the grill. **Serves 2**

Roasted red peppers and aubergines with goat's cheese

20 minutes

roasted red peppers 3 large, drained
soft, mild goat's cheese 125g
grilled aubergines in oil 150g, drained
semi-dried tomatoes 4, chopped
(try Merchant Gourmet, either
Mi-Cuit or SunBlush)
basil leaves a handful, torn
rocket
extra-virgin olive oil
balsamic vinegar
ciabatta or bruschettini toasted, to serve

■ Slice each red pepper in half and spread each piece with goat's cheese. Top with a slice of aubergine, some tomato and basil. Season with salt and pepper and roll up.
■ Divide the pepper rolls between 2 plates. Add the rocket and drizzle with olive oil and balsamic vinegar. Serve with toasted ciabatta or bruschettini.
Serves 2

Find roasted red peppers and grilled aubergines at deli counters or in jars (Karyatis is a good brand).

Creamy herb and bean pasta

20 minutes

garganelli (small, ridged pasta tubes) or
    penne 350g
olive oil
garlic 1 clove, crushed
runner beans a handful, trimmed and
    sliced
peas 350g
mint a small bunch, chopped
parsley a small handful, chopped
soft goat's cheese 150g, crumbled
crème fraîche 100ml
pine nuts 2 tbsp, toasted
Pecorino cheese 25g, shaved

■ Cook the pasta according to the packet instructions. Meanwhile, heat 2 tbsp olive oil in a frying pan, add the garlic and beans, and cook gently for about 10 minutes until starting to soften. Add the peas, mint, parsley, goat's cheese and crème fraîche, season and cook until melted into a creamy sauce. Toss the pasta with the sauce and serve topped with the pine nuts and Pecorino. **Serves 4**

If runner beans aren't in season, you could use frozen broad beans.

Spaghetti al pomodoro with greens and mozzarella

30 minutes

---

garlic 5 cloves, finely chopped

olive oil

peeled plum tomatoes 2 × 400g tins

spaghetti 400g

kale or other greens such as spinach
    200g, chopped

mozzarella cheese 1 ball, ripped into
    large chunks

■ Cook the garlic in 3 tbsp olive oil until golden. Pour in the tomatoes, break up slightly with a spoon and season. Cook for 15 minutes until the sauce is thick.

■ Cook the pasta following packet instructions. In the last 3 minutes of cooking, add the greens. Drain, add to the sauce and mozzarella and mix. **Serves 4**

You can use 8 large, fresh tomatoes, skinned, instead of the tinned, if you like.

Courgette and herb risotto

40 minutes

butter 50g
courgettes 4, sliced into thin strips
  lengthways
olive oil
shallots 3 or 1 onion, finely chopped
garlic 2 cloves, finely chopped
risotto rice 400g, preferably carnaroli
dry white wine 150ml
hot vegetable stock fresh, cube or
  powder, made up to 1.5 litres, kept
  simmering in a pan
chives and flat-leaf parsley 1 bunch of
  each, chopped
Parmesan cheese 25g, grated

Look for carnaroli risotto rice as it is
easier to cook and get right.

■ Heat a large frying pan. Add a third of
the butter. When it's foaming add the
courgettes. Fry for a few minutes each
side until golden. Drain off any excess fat
and keep warm.

■ Heat a large heavy-based saucepan and
add 1 tbsp olive oil and another third of
butter. Heat until it is foaming, then add
the shallots and cook for 5 minutes or
until they begin to soften. Add the garlic,
then stir in the rice and heat through for
a minute until it is completely coated and
shiny. Pour in the wine and bubble,
stirring until it evaporates. Reduce the
heat to medium and add the stock a
ladleful at a time, allowing the liquid to
be absorbed into the rice before adding
more. This will take up to 20 minutes.

■ When the rice feels soft, but still has
a little bite and the texture is creamy,
the risotto is ready. Take it off the heat
and stir in the herbs, Parmesan and
remaining butter. Season. Spoon the
courgettes on top. **Serves 4**

Spinach and mushroom pilaf

30 minutes

onions 2, finely sliced
garlic 2 cloves, crushed
butter 50g
chestnut mushrooms 150g, sliced
cinnamon 1 stick
cloves 4 whole
cardamom pods 4, bruised
basmati rice 250g
lemon ½, zested and juiced
vegetable stock fresh, cube or
    concentrate, made up to 450ml
spinach 200g, washed and roughly
    chopped

■ Cook the onion and garlic in the butter in a large, shallow pan until soft and golden. Add the mushrooms and cook until softened. Add the spices and cook for 2 minutes, then stir in the rice, lemon zest and stock. Cover. Cook on a gentle heat for about 15 minutes until the liquid has been absorbed. Stir through the spinach and lemon juice, cover for 2 minutes until wilted and serve. **Serves 4**

Marigold Bouillon, which is sold in tubs, makes a really well-flavoured vegetable stock.

Purple-sprouting broccoli pasta

30 minutes

linguine 400g
purple-sprouting broccoli 400g,
    roughly chopped
garlic 3–4 cloves, finely sliced
dried red chillies 2–3, chopped
olive oil
ricotta cheese 250g

■ Bring a large saucepan of water to the boil and add the linguine. After 4 minutes, add the broccoli and cook until the pasta is *al dente* (about another 7 minutes); the broccoli should be quite tender by now. Drain both, reserving a couple of tablespoons of the cooking water.

■ Fry the garlic and chilli in 2 tbsp olive oil until the garlic begins to brown. Add this to the pasta and mix well. Season with freshly ground black pepper and sea salt. Add the ricotta in blobs, but don't stir in completely – that way, you'll get creamy hits as you eat. **Serves 4**

Purple-sprouting broccoli is the trendier cousin of broccoli – you can eat it all, so chop the stalks and leaves too.

Courgette and ricotta cannelloni

30 minutes

onion 1, chopped
olive oil
courgettes 4, grated
garlic 2 cloves, crushed
lemon 1, zested
ricotta cheese 250g carton
Parmesan cheese 50g, grated
passata, sugocasa or tomato pasta sauce
    700g jar
fresh lasagne sheets 1 packet, about 250g

■ Heat the oven to 200°C/fan 180°C/gas 6. Fry the onion in 2 tbsp olive oil until soft. Add the courgette and garlic, cook until soft. Off the heat, stir in the zest and half of each cheese. Season.

■ Pour half the tomato sauce into a baking dish. Spread the courgette mixture down the centre of each lasagne sheet and roll into tubes. Lay on top of the sauce, seam-side down. Pour over the rest of the passata, dot with the remaining cheese. Bake for 15 minutes until golden. **Serves 4**

Lasagne sheets come in different sizes, so you may have to trim some of the larger ones.

Halloumi wrapped in red pepper with lemon and chilli

30 minutes

red peppers 4
halloumi cheese 200g block, sliced into 4
lemon 1, zested and juiced
red chilli 1, finely chopped
oregano fresh, chopped to make 2 tsp or
    1 tsp dried
black or green olives 4, cut into slivers

To make this even quicker, buy grilled
whole peppers from a deli.

■ Grill the red peppers whole until they begin to soften (if you like them skinned, keep going until you can skin them). You need them soft enough to wrap the cheese but not too soft or you won't be able to cook them again.

■ Open out each red pepper by making a cut down one side and trim the tops and bottoms off so you end up with a strip. Put a slice of halloumi in the centre of each strip. Sprinkle over some lemon zest and juice, divide the chilli, oregano and olives among them, then roll the red pepper around the halloumi. It doesn't matter if the cheese sticks out at each end. Tie the rolls with some kitchen string that you have soaked in water (or secure with a cocktail stick) and press down with the palm of your hand so they flatten slightly.

■ Grill or char-grill the red peppers on both sides for 5 minutes or until they are starting to char and the cheese is softening and browning at the ends (keep an eye on the string as it could burn off). **Serves 4**

Tomato, cauliflower and spinach curry

30 minutes

onion 1, sliced
oil 2 tbsp
curry paste 2 tbsp
cauliflower 1 small, cut into bite-sized florets
plum tomatoes 400g tin
spinach 100g, roughly chopped
naan bread to serve

■ Fry the onion in the oil until soft and golden – about 7 minutes. Add the curry paste and cook for a couple of minutes until fragrant. Throw in the cauliflower, tomato and 300ml water then bring to a gentle simmer for 10–15 minutes until the tomato has broken down and the cauliflower is tender.

■ Stir through the spinach until wilted and serve with warm naan bread.

Serves 2

You can use any curry paste: Rogan Josh is one with a good flavour.

Pappardelle with leeks and shiitake mushrooms

15 minutes

pappardelle or tagliatelle 150g
olive oil
shiitake mushrooms 150g, sliced
leeks 3, washed and sliced
garlic 3 cloves, crushed
truffle oil 2 tbsp, available from delis and
    some supermarkets
Parmesan cheese 2 tbsp, freshly grated,
    plus extra for serving

■ Cook the pasta following the packet instructions. Meanwhile, heat 2 tbsp olive oil in a large frying pan and cook the mushrooms, leeks and garlic until soft and just beginning to brown.
Season with plenty of salt and freshly ground pepper.
■ Drain the pasta, reserving about 4 tbsp of the cooking water. Mix the water, vegetables and pasta together, then trickle over 1 tbsp truffle oil. Stir briefly, then scatter over the Parmesan and toss to combine. Divide between 2 plates and drizzle over the rest of the truffle oil. Serve with extra Parmesan.
Serves 2

Don't just save truffle oil for special occasions. Keep a bottle in the fridge and use it to glam up soups, risotto or even mashed potato.

Cheddar, onion and potato plate pies

30 minutes

ready-rolled shortcrust pastry 1 sheet
potatoes 2 large, halved and sliced
spring onions 6, sliced
butter
double cream 142ml carton
mature Cheddar cheese 50g, grated
egg 1, whisked, to glaze

■ Heat the oven to 220°C/fan 200°C/gas 7. Cut two circles, large enough to cover two small, ovenproof plates, from the pastry. Boil the potatoes for 5 minutes. Meanwhile, fry the onions in a little butter until soft, then add the cream and cheese and stir until melted. Drain the potatoes, then stir into the cheese mix.
■ Divide between the 2 plates, brush the edges with a little egg, then cover with the pastry circles. Crimp the edges, glaze all over with egg and bake for 15 minutes. Serve with green vegetables or a salad. **Serves 2**

Look out for Jus-Rol All Butter pastry in the freezer section. It has a great flavour.

Strawberries with vanilla ice cream, black pepper and whisky

5 minutes

strawberries 200g, sliced
vanilla ice cream 4 scoops
whisky 4 tsp
clear honey 2 tsp
whole black pepper freshly grated

■ Pile the strawberries and ice cream into 2 bowls, sprinkling with whisky and drizzling honey as you go. Alternatively, layer in 2 whisky tumblers. Grind over a little black pepper and serve. **Serves 2**

Elsanta is the most widely available strawberry, but look out for other, more highly flavoured varieties such as Florence, Alice, Rose or Rhapsody.

Caramel cherry cream

20 minutes

cherries 450g, pitted
cherry liqueur or brandy 2 tbsp
mascarpone 250g
orange 1, zested
double cream 284ml carton
amaretti biscuits 12
golden granulated sugar 100g

■ Tip the cherries and liqueur into a bowl and leave to soak. Beat the mascarpone with the orange zest. Whip the double cream and fold it into the mascarpone.
■ Put the biscuits in a large glass dish. Layer the cherries and cream mixture on top, ending with a layer of cream. Heat the sugar in a frying pan until it starts to melt. Swirl it around as it starts to caramelise to keep the colour even. Once it reaches a deep gold colour, pour it on to the cream – it may bubble as you do so. Be careful not to pour it straight into the glass or it may shatter. **Serves 4–6**

Fresh cherries are perfect for this. Get yourself a cherry pitter, and it will take no time at all. They're available from good kitchenware stores.

Fruit and oat crumbles

30 minutes

porridge oats 100g
rye or bran flakes 75g
caster sugar 75g
unsalted butter 100g, softened
clear honey 2 tbsp
blueberries 200g
bananas 2–3 ripe, sliced
lemon 1, juice
light muscovado sugar 50g

Ramekins or ring moulds work
for this recipe. Buy ring moulds at
good kitchenware shops or
www.divertimenti.co.uk

■ Heat the oven to 180°C/fan 160°C/gas 4.
Put the oats and rye flakes in a bowl.
Melt the caster sugar, butter and honey
in a saucepan. Stir into the oat mixture.
Lightly butter a large baking sheet (don't
butter if using ramekins). Put six 7–8cm
round, bottomless ring moulds or
6 buttered 200ml ramekins on the baking
sheet. Spoon the oat mixture into each
ring or ramekin, pressing it down.

■ Combine the blueberries, banana and
lemon juice, then stir in the muscovado
sugar. Spoon on to the oat base. Bake for
15 minutes until the fruit is soft.

■ Cool for 2 minutes. Slide each mould on
to a plate, run a knife around the mould's
edge and lift it off. If using ramekins,
serves as they are. Great with ice cream.
Serves 6

Dime bar dreams

10 minutes

Dime bars (or **Snickers**, if you prefer)
   about 100g
double cream 284ml carton
caster sugar 1 tbsp
bananas 2, sliced
Tia Maria (optional)

■ Break up the Dime bars before you unwrap them by hitting them with a rolling pin. Remove the wrappers. Whip the cream and sugar together until very soft peaks form. Fold in half the banana slices and half the crushed Dime bars.

■ Divide among 4 small serving glasses or bowls. Top with the remaining bananas and crushed Dime bars. Pour on a slug of Tia Maria, if you fancy.

Serves 4

You can pick up big bags of Dime bars at IKEA.

Instant apple tarts

20 minutes

red-skinned dessert apples 3 small

fruit bread or brioche 4 large or 8 small
slices

unsalted butter ¼ of a 250g packet

ground cinnamon 1–2 tsp

light muscovado sugar 4 tsp

vanilla pod 2, cut in half and then halved
lengthways

■ Heat the oven to 200°C/fan 180°C/gas 6.
Core and quarter the apples. Slice thinly.

■ Trim the bread into rectangles. If using
4 large slices, cut in half to produce
8 rectangles and generously butter one
side of each. Put on a buttered baking
sheet butter side up.

■ Arrange the apple slices on the bread
and sprinkle with cinnamon and sugar.
Dot with the remaining butter and
top with the vanilla pods. Bake for
6–10 minutes or until the apples are
just cooked and the bread toasted.
Serve with ice cream, cream or custard.

Serves 4

Worcester Pearmain and Laxton's apples
look best, but any dessert apples will do.
For a pâtisserie-like finish, brush with
honey when cooked.

Chocolate pots with cherry compote

10 minutes + 20 minutes chilling

plain chocolate 100g, chopped
double cream 284ml carton
vanilla extract 1 tsp
cherry compote 4 rounded tbsp (Bonne
  Maman is good)
biscuits (such as biscotti or tuiles)
  to serve

■ Melt the chocolate in a microwave or in a bowl over a pan of hot water and stir until smooth. Don't let any water get in the chocolate as that will spoil it.

■ Add the cream and vanilla extract and a pinch of salt. Mix thoroughly. Divide between 4 small espresso cups or ramekins and chill for 20 minutes. Spoon the cherry compote on top and serve with a few biscuits. **Serves 4**

Serve these with posh biscuits, but nothing too chunky.

Raspberry trifle

20 minutes + chilling

Madeira cake 250g, cubed
raspberries 300g
blackcurrant and raspberry liqueur
   200ml
orange 1, zest grated
custard 300g carton
double cream 142ml carton
flaked almonds a handful, lightly toasted

■ Tip the cake cubes into a trifle bowl
or 6 glasses. Mix most of the raspberries
(keep just a few for decoration) with
the liqueur. Spread them over the cake,
crushing them slightly as you do so.
■ Mix the orange zest into the custard.
Leave to stand for 5 minutes then
carefully pour the custard over the
raspberries in an even layer.
■ Whip the cream lightly and spoon over
the custard. Chill until needed. Just before
serving, decorate with the remaining
raspberries and some flaked almonds.
Serves 6

Use trifle sponges rather than Madeira
cake, if you like.

Mars bar cups with toasted marshmallows

25 minutes

double cream 284ml carton
Mars bars 200g, chopped
cognac 2½ tbsp
butter a knob of
marshmallows 6, toasted

■ Heat the double cream in a pan to simmering point. Turn the heat down low and add the Mars bars, stirring until smooth. Remove from the heat and stir in the cognac and a knob of butter.

■ Skewer each marshmallow on a cocktail stick and carefully toast over a gas flame. Divide the Mars bar mix among 6 espresso cups. Serve warm topped with a toasted marshmallow.

Serves 6

If you are serving this to kids then leave out the cognac.

Papaya with chilli caramel

15 minutes

light muscovado sugar 4 tbsp
red chilli 1 small, deseeded, cut into
    thin strips
lime 1, zest in strips and juice
papaya 1 ripe, skin removed

■ Put the sugar, chilli and 100ml water in a pan and bring to the boil. Simmer for 5 minutes to make a light syrup. Stir in the lime zest and juice, pour into a jug and cool.
■ Cut the papaya into thin wedges and arrange on plates. Pour over the syrup and serve. **Serves 2**

Papaya should look yellowish and feel slightly yielding to the touch when ripe.

Banoffee fool

15 minutes

digestive biscuits 6 plain
butter 25g, melted
bananas 2 large ripe
lemon juice 1 tbsp
Carnation Caramel or Banoffee Toffee
    5 tbsp
double cream 142ml carton
custard 200ml
chocolate curls to decorate

The easiest way to make chocolate curls is to stand a block of chocolate upright on a board and peel curls down the block with a swivel potato peeler.

■ Put the biscuits in a strong food bag and bash them up with a rolling pin. Mix with the melted butter. Slice the bananas and mix with the lemon juice and caramel or toffee. Whip the cream until it just holds its shape, then fold in the custard.

■ Spoon 1 tbsp of the biscuit crumbs into the base of each of 4 tumblers, spoon over half the banoffee mix, then half the custard mix. Repeat these layers, reserving a few crumbs for the top. Sprinkle the top of each fool with remaining biscuit crumbs and chocolate curls. Chill until ready to serve. **Serves 4**

Index

Picture credits and recipe credits

BBC Books would like to thank the following for providing photographs. While every effort has been made to trace and acknowledge all photographers, we would like to apologize should there be any errors or omissions.

Marie-Louise Avery p73, p83, p113, p115, p197, p199; Iain Bagwell p29, p209; Peter Cassidy p5 (right), p6, p53, p59, p77, p85, p95, p97, p105, p125, p153, p155, p159, p165, p177, p179, p201, p211; Jean Cazals p25, p35; Brent Darby p4 (middle), p75, Dan Duchars p13; Lisa Linder p23, p71; Jason Lowe p15, p55, p57, p141, p151, p175, p187, p191; David Munns p4 (left), p19, p37, p47, p63, p101, p107, p119, p133, p171, p203, p207; Noel Murphy p111; Myles New p4 (right), p33, p45, p89, p91, p93, p103, p129, p149, p161; Roger Stowell p11, p21, p51, p61, p65, p69, p81, p123, p139, p145, p169, p173, p181, p183, p189, p193, p195; Simon Walton p17, p31, p79, p137, p163; Philip Webb p5 (left, middle), p27, p39, p41, p43, p49, p67, p87, p99, p117, p121, p127, p131, p135, p143, p147, p157, p167, p185, p205, p209.

All the recipes in this book have been created by the editorial team at BBC *olive* magazine.